SelectScripts

About the Authors

Paul and Nicole Johnson share their lives on stage, reflecting real-life experiences that touch the deep-seated needs of those who see them perform.

In over ten years of full-time acting, Paul and Nicole have performed at universities, churches, conventions, and conferences before an estimated audience of more than one million. They have been featured on national television programs such as "Crook and Chase," "The 700 Club," and Canada's "Open House." They also have appeared at Focus on the Family "Life on the Edge" events and "Aspiring Women" conferences.

Paul and Nicole are the authors of *Random Acts of Grace* book and audio book, as well as several collections of their dramatic sketches. They are winners of an Angel Award for their video, *To Have to Hold*.

For more information about the performance ministry of Paul and Nicole Johnson, visit our web site at **www.paulandnicole.com** or contact:

Backstage Booking
P.O. Box 3027
Brentwood, TN 37024
(615) 661-0220
FAX: (615) 661-5222

Other Resources Available from Paul and Nicole Johnson

Random Acts of Grace Paperback Book and Audio Book (published by Broadman and Holman)
To Have and to Hold Video Cassette
Extreme and *2 Extreme* Youth Musical and Songbook
SelectScripts Volume 2 (Youth and Family)
SelectScripts Volume 3 (Parables)

Call 888-74-DRAMA to order.

SelectScripts

BY PAUL & NICOLE JOHNSON

VOLUME 1

M A R R I A G E

BROADMAN
& HOLMAN
PUBLISHERS

Nashville, Tennessee

© 1995, 1999 by Paul and Nicole Johnson.
SelectScripts is a trademark of Paul and Nicole Johnson.

0-8054-2023-1

Published in 1999 by Broadman & Holman, Nashville, Tennessee

Dewey Decimal Classification: 246
Subject Heading: DRAMATIC SCRIPTS
Library of Congress Card Catalog Number: 98-56165

IMPORTANT: Permission to perform the sketches in this *SelectScripts* volume (Performance Rights), by amateur groups or individuals only, is granted with the purchase of this *SelectScripts* volume. Any performance by a professional group (receiving compensation through honorariums or offerings) requires written permission from Paul and Nicole Johnson and a $100.00 licensing fee per script, renewable annually.

Only original purchaser is granted photocopy permission.

All other rights reserved. Printed in the United States of America.

Unless otherwise noted, Scripture quotations are from the Holy Bible, New International Version, copyright © 1973, 1978, 1984 by International Bible Society. Also quoted is NASB, the New American Standard Bible, © the Lockman Foundation, 1960, 1962, 1963, 1968, 1971, 1972, 1973, 1975, 1977; used by permission.

Library of Congress Cataloging-in-Publication Data

Johnson, Paul, 1966–
    SelectScripts / by Paul and Nicole Johnson.
        p.   cm.
    Includes bibliographical references.
    Contents: v. 1. Marriage — v. 2. Youth and family — v. 3. Parables.
    ISBN 0-8054-2023-1 (v. 1). — ISBN 0-8054-2024-X (v. 2). — ISBN 0-8054-2025-8 (v. 3)
    1. Drama in Christian education. 2. Christian drama, American.
I. Johnson, Nicole, 1966– . II. Title. III. Title: Select scripts.

BV1534.4.J66   1999
246' .72—dc21   98-56165
                                                                                                                                                CIP

4 5 6 04 03 02 01

Contents

Preface . . . . *vii*
Introduction: A Proper Preparation 1
The Lost Key 5
    Plot: A man discovers how an issue from his past affects his marriage today.
    Characters: 5 (2 male adults, 1 female adult, 1 male teen, 1 boy)
    Time: 6–7 minutes
    Theme: Dealing with the past, forgiveness, unconditional love

Marriage on the Run 11
    Plot: A humorous, yet poignant look at a couple's busy lives and the toll it takes on their marriage and family.
    Characters: 2 (1 male adult, 1 female adult)
    Time: 8 minutes
    Theme: Busyness, making time for each other

Our Night Out 19
    Plot: A married couple's near "date night" disaster.
    Characters: 2 (1 male adult, 1 female adult)
    Time: 3–4 minutes
    Theme: Marital dating, being together

We Are So Different 23
    Plot: A couple enjoys their differences early in their marriage and then finds themselves enduring those differences on the road to embracing them.
    Characters: 2 (1 female adult, 1 male adult)
    Time: 9 minutes
    Theme: Differences, honoring each other, mutual submission

Scripts 31
    Plot: A couple gives their story to a "Scripts Anonymous" group, revealing those fights they find themselves arguing again and again.
    Characters: 2 (1 female adult, 1 male adult)
    Time: 7 minutes
    Theme: Communication, intimacy, the ability to change

Contents

The Ledger People 37
    Plot: Since keeping a ledger is good for finances, a couple believes it is the answer for "keeping score" on each other.
    Characters: 2 (1 male adult, 1 female adult)
    Time: 8 minutes
    Theme: Love, grace, forgiveness

One Flesh 45
    Plot: A scriptural medley on love and marriage.
    Characters: 2 (1 male adult, 1 female adult)
    Time: 5–6 minutes
    Theme: Love, marriage

Hidden Anger 51
    Plot: Unresolved anger in a woman's life nearly destroys her marriage.
    Characters: 2 (1 male adult, 1 female adult)
    Time: 11 minutes
    Theme: Anger, forgiveness

Preface

Welcome to the first volume of *SelectScripts*. We hope the features of this scriptbook will help you and your drama team in your preparation to present quality sketches. We have tried to provide information that will assist you in your script choices, rehearsals, and team development. We have included a rating system for the sketches: on a scale from one to ten, one being the easiest and ten presenting the most challenges. We have performed all of these sketches in various settings and are passing along our notes and thoughts on what we've discovered works well for each piece. Feel free to heed or ignore the advice. The goal is to help you connect with your audience.

We have been married since 1987, and though none of the sketches in this marriage volume are autobiographical, they do have their roots in our lives and relationship. We have wrestled (and still do) with many of these issues in an ongoing effort to understand our own brokenness as we move toward each other in love. We hope the sketches in this book will challenge your relationships as well as help you serve your community by raising tough questions.

Grace to you,
Paul and Nicole Johnson

Introduction: A Proper Preparation

Effective drama teams and theatrical companies hold this truth to be self-evident: Drama has as much potential to impact its actors as it does to impact the world. But there is a trend in our churches to use drama as a piece of "the formula" for growing a "successful" church. This trend can lead to shallow, lifeless pieces. Drama has the power to touch the world, but it must first touch the dramatic artist.

More time must be given to the rehearsal process. Often, the tendency is to gather the team days before the presentation, hand out scripts, quickly memorize lines, run through the piece a couple of times to get a sense of blocking, and then perform. No time is given to digest the piece, extract its meanings, or experiment with its presentation. The result? Flat, bad drama that the audience dismisses as irrelevant.

In college we first discovered a textbook entitled *Acting One* by Robert Cohen. In his introduction, he wrote of six preliminary things that would be helpful for the beginning actor to know. We find them to be at the actual core of team dynamics and the foundation for the rehearsal process in order to connect the artists to one another, to the work, and to the audience. The six preliminaries for transforming your drama group into a powerful ministry team are relaxation, trust, discipline, criticism, freedom, and preparation.

Relaxation

Start with relaxation, the conduit for creativity. Without it, ideas are stifled, emotions squelched, the body restricted, and relationships dampened. The actor comes to rehearsal with the cares of the world on his shoulders, and this burden is too weighty. An actor must be fresh, or the rehearsal time is doomed before it begins. Therefore, transition into each rehearsal time with some buffer activities to provide a release for the actors. For example, have some nice music playing for the actors as they arrive, and encourage them to begin to unwind with some simple stretching exercises to relieve physical tension. Have your team warm up by lightly bouncing up and down or shaking their limbs. Light exercise does wonders to induce relaxation.

The team also requires mental relaxation, putting off all of the day-to-day affairs that crowd their thoughts and create tension. Actors cannot focus on their characters and their dramatic situations when they are preoccupied with the business of their everyday lives. Actors may achieve mental relaxation by breathing deeply and "letting go" of their worries. Then, they can begin to focus on the present and the task at hand. They may want to pray or quote Scripture silently, thinking on things that are honorable, true, and noble. Relaxing mentally is really about becoming open and receptive without being preoccupied, worried, and self-centered.

Relaxation opens the door to creativity. Simple exercises, mental and physical, provide ample space for transition from the outside world to the creative world. It also tills the soil for the next preliminary, trust.

Trust

Having oneself on display requires a great deal of vulnerability in front of an audience. Vulnerability is nurtured in rehearsal with one's teammates. Being able to make a fool of oneself in rehearsal without being shamed or embarrassed, or being able to reveal deep emotions and sensitivities without being stepped on is crucial to rehearsal. If inner character workings cannot be exposed in rehearsal, they will not be exposed on stage.

Trust is built in relationships by mutual caring, sharing, and common concern. It first begins in the relaxed self that feels confident and comfortable, and is further developed by the common experiences of the group. Simple trust exercises and games work well, as well as giving back rubs, sharing needs and praying together, and socializing as a group outside of rehearsal. Trust is established over time as the group interacts sensibly and sensitively with one another. Treat one another with care. Be able to apologize genuinely when an offense has occurred.

Neither trust nor relaxation come automatically. Everyone brings different fears and tensions to rehearsal and performance. The more you acknowledge those fears and tensions, the more you will be able to respond to your team with less anger and irritation. You can enter the creative world with hope, authenticity, and fullness of spirit. A good drama team needs to relax with and trust one another, and discipline plays a primary role in accomplishing these.

Discipline

Theater is a collaborative art and requires the involvement and input of many people. Discipline becomes mandatory for *all* participants. Without discipline, there will be no trust. If an actor cannot be trusted to follow through with his responsibilities (being on time, knowing his lines, etc.), how can he be trusted to respect others' vulnerabilities?

Enjoying the theatrical process becomes a reality through the dedication and commitment of each individual to interact responsibly with one another on a continual basis. Trust flourishes in a disciplined atmosphere because actors can count on one another.

Discipline also enables the artist to take his craft to the next level. It deepens the work as the actor applies himself to learning more of the art form, more of the script, more of the purpose, and more about himself. Discipline develops within him a teachable spirit. And it invites the next preliminary, criticism.

Criticism

The proper criticism, given in a relaxed, trustworthy, and safe environment, builds up and makes better. What makes criticism so difficult is the fact that the dramatic artist is the one on display. The art is so closely tied to the person. Most of us, in such a vulnerable position, want and need affirmation. It is hard not to take the criticism personally. Unfortunately, criticism is not given from only your team. Every audience member is a critic, and many want to be sure their opinions are heard. And those opinions often sting.

Remember, your identity does not depend on the opinions of others. Filter criticism. Consider the source, and if the person proves trustworthy, pay attention to every detail. In other situations, try to find the nugget of criticism that is truthful and helpful. In the end, all criticism remains subjective analysis. You will not be able to please everyone. Learn what you can and move on. Turn the critique to your advantage and, with discipline, keep moving toward growth, comfort on stage, and greater freedom in performance. The best actors do not avoid criticism; they invite it. The more willing you are to engage discipline and criticism, the better your work will be. And the more power it will possess to impact the audience and the artist.

Freedom

A good actor pursues the goal of freedom: freedom of movement and mind, but primarily, freedom of imagination. Since drama is a world of the imagination, the bigger that world for the individual actor, the more room to move. And the more an actor moves in his imagination, the more he will find what connects him to his character, to the sketch or play, and to the audience.

The actor's imagination must be unhindered. He must be free to think, feel, receive, give, experiment, fail, create, touch, and be touched. The free actor is unencumbered by fear. Fear of rejection is his worst enemy. A good actor courageously exposes what is true and real in the script. All art is risky because it involves telling the truth. Sometimes the truth is rejected, but Scripture does not allow fear as an excuse for not telling the truth.

The other preliminaries play a part in freedom. Relaxation and trust enable the actor to move unhindered by stress and relational inhibitions; discipline establishes a safe environment in which to move; criticism allows the actor to grow from his experiences. Each of these is essential to create a space where freedom reigns.

More time for rehearsal must be set aside in order for freedom to become a part of the actors' lives and work. Freedom will not be found in "hit and run" theater. The quality and depth of your pieces depend on it. This leads us to the last preliminary for great team dynamics and outstanding presentation.

Preparation

Developing a strong team demands more than "token" rehearsals. Cohesiveness of your group will not be secured by just spending time together in rehearsal and performance. Other activities that the group can do together will inspire their creativity and encourage their growth. For instance, taking a dance class together can go a long way toward building team unity. Dance remains an excellent source of movement, timing, and rhythm training. Athletics builds teamwork and awareness of energy demands on the body. Singing, poetry reading, writing, and storytelling stretch language and articulation skills. Reading all types of books expands the mind and fosters an overall understanding of humanity. And, of course, theatergoing rates high as a source of inspiration. Seeing the work of another team firsthand, learning from their creativity and expression, serve as reminders of the impact that theater has on the soul.

These preliminaries to acting—relaxation, trust, discipline, response to criticism, freedom of imagination, and participating in other skills for personal and team preparation—are developed over time as artists commit themselves to the work and world of the theater.

Resources for further reading

Cohen, Robert. *Acting One.* Irvine, Calif.: Mayfield Publishing Co., 1984.
———. *Acting Power.* Irvine, Calif.: Mayfield Publishing Co., 1978.
Hagen, Uta. *Respect for Acting.* New York: MacMillan Publishing Co., 1973.
———. *A Challenge for the Actor.* New York: MacMillan Publishing Co., 1991.

The Lost Key

In our book, *Random Acts of Grace,* there is a story called "The Coach." It is about a woman who finds herself overwhelmed with activity to make herself acceptable. She laments, "My husband, my mother, my pastor, and all my friends could love and accept me, but I would still want more . . . , because *I* don't accept me. And I know that if there is one person on this planet who doesn't love me, then I will side with that person because that's how I feel about myself."

The pursuit of success, popularity, or power are ways to avoid intimacy. People remind us of how defective we feel. If marriage is about the giving of ourselves to another and deep down we believe that we are a defective gift, then naturally we will be quite hesitant to give ourselves to our spouses. This creates a marriage of isolation, loneliness, and resentment.

We desperately need the grace and love of God. Our hope of loving another is rooted in being loved at our core by the only one who can love us that way. That deep, unconditional love will not be found in any other person, especially our spouse. "The Lost Key" implores us to turn to the Heavenly Father for the deep love and grace that sets us free from the pursuit and enables us to enter into our relationships fully.

Production Notes

Theme: Dealing with the past, forgiveness, unconditional love
Target Audience: Families, married adults
Degree of Difficulty: 8 (includes heavy emotional content)
Running Time: 6–7 minutes
Characters: BILL, late twenties or early thirties
BETH, late twenties or early thirties
FATHER of Bill
BOY 1, Bill as a boy
BOY 2, Bill as a teenager
Setting: Scene 1: Kitchen of BILL and BETH's home
Scene 2: The school grounds
Scene 3: At the ballpark
Scene 4: Kitchen of BILL and BETH's home

Props: 2 kitchen chairs
Kitchen table

General Notes: Everything about this sketch is intense. From the opening argument through the second flashback scene (sc. 3), BILL and his childhood characters struggle for control. Finally in the last scene, when he admits what is really going on within him, the weight of the piece begins to lift.

Nicole plays the FATHER in the flashbacks as a voice only. He does not need to be a physical presence on stage. In fact, it might be distracting if he is. Paul plays the boy and the teenager in scenes 2 and 3.

Scene 1 *(BILL and his wife, BETH, in their kitchen)*

BILL: Honey, what's wrong?
BETH: Nothing.
BILL: Now, I know that when you say "nothing" that your nothing definitely means something.
BETH: It's nothing, just drop it.
BILL: Are you mad at me?
BETH: I'm not mad at you. I'm just disappointed.
BILL: Don't be disappointed, I just forgot.
BETH: That's what you always say.
BILL: I said I was sorry.
BETH: I'm sure you are.
BILL: Now what does that mean?
BETH: It means that you always say you're sorry, but you always forget important things, and I don't see you making any effort to remember them.
BILL: I remember things. Do you think we would be in the house we are in, or I'd have the job that I have, if I couldn't remember anything?
BETH: OK, I exaggerated. It's the little things.
BILL: Like what?
BETH: Like two weeks ago when I asked you to stop by the grocery store on your way home, or two days ago when I needed you to pick up Katie from Mother's Day Out, or yesterday when you were supposed to call your sister about the lawn mower in the garage, or tonight when the Joneses had been in our living room for one solid hour before you remembered we were having company and decided to come home—
BILL: OK, OK!
BETH: Bill, why can't you remember?

BILL:	Well, maybe if you didn't get so mad at me I could remember!
BETH:	I'm not mad!
BILL:	Oh? Well, then let's try "disappointed." Do you know how sick and tired I get of disappointing you? I don't think I can do anything right. I might as well admit it. I'm stupid, I'm dumb. I can't remember anything.
BETH:	Why are you saying that?
BILL:	Because it's true, obviously. (*pause*) All right, if you must know, I got turned down for that promotion that came up again at work.
BETH:	Honey, why didn't you tell me?
BILL:	Don't say that, Beth. You are the first one to get your hopes up and then be disappointed in me. I'm not Superman—and I get sick and tired of never living up to your expectations. You're always (*mimics her*) so disappointed in me.
BETH:	That's not what I meant, and you know it!
BILL:	Yes it is. You're just like my father!
BETH:	What are you talking about?
BILL:	You're just like my father and this is just like that key, that stupid key....

Scene 2
(*BOY 1, Bill as a young boy, and his FATHER late one evening on the school grounds where he works*)

BOY 1:	I don't know where it is.
FATHER:	You lost my key?
BOY 1:	It must have fallen out of my pocket.
FATHER:	You stupid kid!
BOY 1:	I'm sorry, Dad. I was just trying—
FATHER:	(*mimics son*) "I'm sorry, I was just . . ."—You are sorry, Son.
BOY 1:	I'll find it, I promise.
FATHER:	You're right, you'll find it. You'll stay out here all night until you find it.
BOY 1:	Yes, Sir.
FATHER:	Now, where was the last place you had it?
BOY 1:	I don't remember. It could have been the B Building....
FATHER:	Think, Son! You have a brain.
BOY 1:	It was the B Building, Dad. Yeah, I was coming out of the B Building and I saw this little kitten—
FATHER:	Don't tell me you stopped to pet a cat. To pet a cat? I don't believe this.
BOY 1:	Yes, Sir, but it was only for a second.
FATHER:	What did I do? What did I do to end up with a son as stupid as you? I knew I should never have given you that key. You lose everything. Now get out there and keep looking.
BOY 1:	But I've already been looking for an hour.
FATHER:	Did you find my key?
BOY 1:	No, Sir.

FATHER:	Then get out there and find it!
BOY 1:	But it's cold out and it's getting dark.
FATHER:	What did I tell you to do, Son?
BOY 1:	Can't we just come back and look for it tomorrow?
FATHER:	No wonder you do bad in school. Just go home and get out of my sight!
BOY 1:	Well, let me get my jacket and a light.
FATHER:	What did I tell you to do?
BOY 1:	I want to look one more time—
FATHER:	What did I tell you to do, Son? Are you deaf too?

Scene 3 (BOY 2, Bill as a teenager, and his FATHER at the ballpark)

FATHER:	What were you thinking out there? What were you *thinking?*
BOY 2:	I don't know.
FATHER:	Of course you don't know! What idiot would think to try to bunt in the last inning with two outs?
BOY 2:	I thought I'd catch them by surprise.
FATHER:	Well, you did that all right. Did your coach tell you to bunt?
BOY 2:	No, Sir.
FATHER:	Of course not. Son, do you realize you got your own man out and lost the game for your team?
BOY 2:	Yes, Sir.
FATHER:	The game!
BOY 2:	Yes, Sir.
FATHER:	What do you think your teammates think of you, Son?
BOY 2:	Not much, Sir.
FATHER:	I'll tell you what they're thinking—they're wondering what they did to end up with the stupidest kid in the world on their team.
BOY 2:	I'm sorry, Dad.
FATHER:	You are sorry, Son.
BOY 2:	(*pause*) Dad?
FATHER:	What?
BOY 2:	I don't think I want to play baseball anymore.
FATHER:	You don't? Because you blew this game you're going to hang it up, is that it? It's not enough for you to humiliate me and your team, but now you want to walk away like a little baby and quit? You are never going to make it in life, Son. I'm telling you now so you won't be surprised. Is that what you want? Answer me!
BOY 2:	No, Sir.
FATHER:	Then I don't want to hear anymore of this quitting garbage. Sometimes I just don't understand you.

Scene 4 *(BILL and BETH in their kitchen)*

BILL: Look, I don't want to talk about it anymore.
BETH: Bill, what's wrong?
BILL: Nothing, it's nothing. Just forget it. It was a bad day at work. I'm sorry I didn't call. I should have let you know that I'd be late. I just needed to drive around for a little while. Just leave me alone for a little while.
BETH: *(pause)* Honey, I'm sorry about the job. I'm sorry if you feel I put pressure on you. I'm sorry for making you angry. It's not that important to get all worked up over.
BILL: I know, I know. I'm just tired. I'm sorry for yelling. Just forget it.
BETH: *(pause)* Bill, what is going on? *(pause)* Please talk to me.
BILL: *(pause, sighs)* I couldn't ever do it, Beth. In school, sports, work—I was just a stupid kid who couldn't remember anything. I never found his key, and . . .
BETH: He never let you forget it.
BILL: *(nods)*
BETH: Honey, that was a long time ago. You were just a little boy.
BILL: I know, but I still feel so stupid sometimes, that I'll never get it right.
BETH: Honey, I'm not your dad. There is no key between us. I love you, and I'm sorry if I haven't communicated that.
BILL: It's not just you. It's everything! I've never known anything different. I guess I never did enough for my dad to love me.
BETH: Never did enough? Would he have loved you if you found his key?
BILL: *(defeated)* Yes.
BETH: Bill, forget the key. You are worth so much to me because of who you are, not for what you do. Thank you for what you do—I'm grateful, but it doesn't determine my love for you. It's like a relationship with God—
BILL: Don't bring God into this.
BETH: Maybe you don't see God's love because of the way your father treated you. Remember, it's not for how we perform, not for what we do, but for who we are that He loves us. There's a big difference.
BILL: *(nods, sighs deeply)*
BETH: Your father needs something from you.
BILL: What?
BETH: Your forgiveness.
BILL: For what?
BETH: For the way he made you feel about yourself. *(pause)* And about God.
BILL: Hmm.
BETH: And I need you to forgive me too.
BILL: For what?
BETH: For going to bed and leaving you with all the dishes.
BILL: Wrong! *(pause, takes her hand)* Thanks.

Opportunities for small group discussion

1. How does how you feel about yourself impact your relationships?
2. How much of what your family of origin said to you in your years together still echoes in your head? How does it affect your current relationships?

Resources for further reading

Allendar, Dan. *The Wounded Heart*. Colorado Springs, Colo.: NavPress, 1990.
Johnson, Paul and Nicole. *Random Acts of Grace*. Nashville: Broadman and Holman, 1998.
Nouwen, Henri. *Life of the Beloved*. New York: The Crossroad Publishing Co., 1992.
Seamonds, David A. *Healing for Damaged Emotions*. Wheaton, Ill.: Victor Books, 1981.
Smalley, Gary, and John Trent. *The Blessing*. New York: Pocket Books, 1986.
Stoop, David. *Making Peace with Your Father*. Wheaton, Ill.: Tyndale House Publishers, 1992.

Marriage on the Run

Life is hectic. Time is a precious commodity. Fast-food restaurants are not fast enough anymore. Our lives can be crazy or calm, and we have the power to choose. We can always be busy, but if we are intentional with our schedules and make time for our marriages, we can still connect with each other.

Production Notes

Theme: Busyness, making time for each other
Target Audience: Married adults
Degree of Difficulty: 7 (This sketch depends on timing, energy, and focus of the characters in quick, short scenes.)
Running Time: 8 minutes
Characters: MAN, husband
WOMAN, wife
Setting: 11 scenes of various settings
Props: 2 chairs, used as various pieces of furniture—a sofa, a bed, etc.
General Notes: This sketch is a series of eleven vignettes that profile a marriage during the course of many years. Each scene builds upon its previous scene. The first scene should communicate more innocence and nervous energy, but not a hectic pace. A sense of busyness and burden grows throughout the following scenes to peak in scene 9. Scene 10 brings the examination of their relationship. Scene 11 demonstrates the fruit of that examination. The challenge for the actors will be to present a "natural" couple that struggles and yet grows together. The timing is critical in that each scene follows directly on the heels of the one before it.

Marriage

Scene 1 (shortly after the wedding)

MAN:	I do.
WOMAN:	I do.
MAN:	You do?
WOMAN:	I do.
MAN:	I do too.
WOMAN:	This is the happiest day of my life.
MAN:	I love you, I love you, I love you, I love you.
WOMAN:	Although, it was a little embarrassing when I said . . .
MAN:	Honey, nobody heard it.
WOMAN:	I was so nervous.
MAN:	You were so beautiful.
WOMAN:	Why are you saying "were"?
MAN:	You still are.
WOMAN:	Thanks.
MAN:	What about me?
WOMAN:	Most handsome man alive.
MAN:	Are you glad you married me?
WOMAN:	I am so glad I married you!

Scene 2 (on their honeymoon)

WOMAN:	I can't believe I married you! I squeeze the toothpaste from the middle, and you squeeze the toothpaste from the bottom!
MAN:	So?
WOMAN:	What a thing to find out on our honeymoon. In all the marriage magazines I've read, they say this is terrible. We'll never make it.
MAN:	I think we'll make it. Remind me to cancel those subscriptions. What do you say we put on our bathing suits, go down to the beach, and work on our tans?
WOMAN:	Well, it would be nice to do some shopping.
MAN:	Shopping? Who comes to the beach on their honeymoon to shop?
WOMAN:	Well, if you go shopping with me, then we could go to that little restaurant we saw on the corner, find a table in the back with a candle, and stare into each other's eyes. . . .
MAN:	Now that's what honeymoons are for!

Scene 3 (*at home*)

MAN: (*on the phone with his mother*) Yep, Mom, the honeymoon is definitely over. I came home tonight, and dinner wasn't anywhere near ready. She even forgot to go by the cleaners. I don't know what she does all day. She said she had been—

WOMAN: (*on the phone with her mother*) to the grocery store. Then to Wal-Mart, the bank, the post office, so I got home late and couldn't get dinner started, and, oh, I forgot to go by the cleaners. He was so—

MAN: mad! I just blew up—I don't know why. It was just a long day at work. I know, I know, that's no reason to get angry. She even started to—

WOMAN: cry. I felt like such a baby. It had been just such a long day. I didn't mean to make him so angry.

MAN: Anyway—

WOMAN: we decided—

TOGETHER: it would never happen again. (*They both hang up the phone.*)

Scene 4 (*at home*)

WOMAN: You said it wouldn't happen again.

MAN: I said I was sorry.

WOMAN: This was supposed to be our night out.

MAN: I know. But the Richards account had to be ready for the morning, so I had to put in some overtime. I'm sorry. I tried to call to let you know I'd be late, but I couldn't get through. Who were you on the phone with for so long?

WOMAN: My mother.

MAN: Your mother? What were you talking to your mother about?

WOMAN: Motherly things.

MAN: Motherly things? Sweetheart, do you realize that's the third time this—

WOMAN: Not since yesterday.

MAN: Since yesterday?

WOMAN: Well . . .

MAN: You called your mother three times today? I can't believe you. We talked about this last month! Sixty percent of our phone bill is to your mother! And during daytime hours! This has got to stop! We simply can't afford it!

WOMAN: Well, I'm sorry, (*volume rises steadily throughout*) but I just needed to talk to her because she was home and you were busy and I was so excited and we planned tonight and talked motherly things and then you were late and I wanted to tell you but you didn't come home so I called again and you finally came home and now it's too late to go out and I had news and now—

MAN: Honey (*trying to interrupt her*), whoa . . . wait . . . I know . . . Honey, whoa . . . (*finally*) BREATHE!!

MARRIAGE

WOMAN:	(*inhales and exhales a big breath*)
MAN:	Sit down. Good grief. OK. Now what is it?
WOMAN:	I'm pregnant.
MAN:	(*shocked, long pause*) You're what?
WOMAN:	Motherly things.
MAN:	(*dazed*) Motherly things?
WOMAN:	Uh-huh.
MAN:	(*pauses, and then explodes*) Well, you should have called *me,* not your mother! Why didn't you call me? I mean, good grief, you're going to have A BABY!
WOMAN:	We're going to have a baby.
MAN:	Right, we're going to have a baby. A son or a daughter—which do we want?
WOMAN:	It doesn't matter.
MAN:	It doesn't matter. . . . A baby . . .
TOGETHER:	It's going to be so wonderful.

Scene 5 (*their bedroom*)

WOMAN:	Oh, wonderful. (*elbows him*) Honey, I know you hear the baby.
MAN:	Mama-moma-uuughn.
WOMAN:	Don't fake it, I know you hear the baby.
MAN:	What baby?
WOMAN:	Your baby.
MAN:	It wasn't my fault.
WOMAN:	OK, it wasn't your fault, but it is your turn.
MAN:	I went at two.
WOMAN:	And I went at three-thirty, and now it's five.
MAN:	In the morning?
WOMAN:	Go get the baby.
MAN:	I'm going, I'm going!

Scene 6 (*at home; pace of the piece starts to pick up here*)

WOMAN:	We're going? Where?
MAN:	Minneapolis! Bill came into my office and laid the offer right on my desk. Twenty percent more money and a big promotion! It was more than I could pass up for you, Jamie, and a second baby on the way.
WOMAN:	But Honey, it's just so sudden.
MAN:	I know, I know, but now we'll be able to do all those things we've always wanted to do.
WOMAN:	In Minneapolis? Do people actually live there?
MAN:	Sure they do. And we will too.
WOMAN:	But it's so far from home.

MAN:	I know, but we'll make a new home. We'll buy a house and find a church and a good school for Jamie. We'll get involved in the community.
WOMAN:	We'll buy a house?
MAN:	Sure we will.

Scene 7 *(in a department store, she is pointing at a chair; the pace quickens.)*

MAN:	Absolutely not!
WOMAN:	But Honey, I like it.
MAN:	Well, I like it, too, but I also like to eat, and we won't be able to do both if we buy that chair.
WOMAN:	Well, I won't eat for a while.
MAN:	Honey, that's not the point.
WOMAN:	No, the point is, you bought golf clubs last week and now I can't buy the chair.
MAN:	Whoa, you wanted those clubs too.
WOMAN:	Until I saw the chair.
MAN:	*(sarcastically)* Well, fine, I'll take the clubs back.
WOMAN:	No! Just let me buy the chair.
MAN:	No, Honey, we just can't afford it.
WOMAN:	How come we can't ever afford what I want?

Scene 8 *(at home; quicker pace)*

MAN:	Honey, I got next Saturday off. Why don't you, me, and the kids go to the zoo and have a picnic?
WOMAN:	I can't. You know that's the church bazaar.
MAN:	The church is bizarre enough; let's go to the zoo.
WOMAN:	I can't, Honey, they're counting on me.

Scene 9 *(at home; getting close to frantic, definitely frazzled)*

WOMAN:	I was really counting on you.
MAN:	I know, I'm sorry, but this business trip came up at the last minute, and there is nothing I can do to get out of it.
WOMAN:	Work gets precedent over a date that we have had scheduled for weeks?
MAN:	We'll do it another time. What about Thursday?
WOMAN:	I have PTA.
MAN:	Friday?
WOMAN:	Little League, and Saturday you're working again.
MAN:	Honey, I'll make it up to you another time. I promise. Don't forget to go by the cleaners.

Marriage

(The pace must pick up during the following until they are shouting at the end, one line on top of the other, but not at each other.)

WOMAN:	Don't forget to pick up Chris after practice and grab supper for you and the kids; I have a late choir rehearsal.
MAN:	I have to leave extra early in the morning, I'm having a breakfast meeting with a client.
WOMAN:	Jamie's sick. Stop by the drug store on your way home to pick up her prescription.
MAN:	I'll be late tonight. I've got a last minute meeting and some final paper work.
WOMAN:	There's a documentary on TV tomorrow night we have to watch for school.
MAN:	I have racquetball with my prayer partner.
WOMAN:	I'm meeting with Chris's teacher.
MAN:	Revival luncheon.
WOMAN:	Grocery shopping.
MAN:	Yard work.
WOMAN:	Homework.
MAN:	Wash the dog.
WOMAN:	Clean the house.
MAN:	In-laws visit.
WOMAN:	Tired.
MAN:	Deacon's meeting.
WOMAN:	Christmas pageant.
MAN:	Father-Daughter Banquet.
WOMAN:	Craft show.
MAN:	I need a break.
WOMAN:	Football game.
MAN:	Office party.
WOMAN:	Holidays.
MAN:	Overtime.
WOMAN:	Shopping.
MAN:	Underpaid.
WOMAN:	Cooking.
MAN:	Eating.
WOMAN:	Cleaning.
MAN:	Fixing.
WOMAN:	Laundry.
MAN:	Papers.
WOMAN:	Vacuuming.
MAN:	Accounts.
WOMAN:	Diapers.
MAN:	Work.
WOMAN:	Grades.

MAN:	More work.
WOMAN:	Kids.
MAN:	Worn out.
WOMAN:	Exhausted.

(*They collapse.*)

Scene 10 (*their bedroom*)

WOMAN:	Good morning.
MAN:	(*barely intelligible*) Good morning.
WOMAN:	I miss you.
MAN:	(*pause*) I miss you too.
WOMAN:	I feel so far apart.
MAN:	We're in the same room.
WOMAN:	I feel so far apart.
MAN:	(*waking up fully*) I know what you mean.
WOMAN:	What's happening to us?
MAN:	What's happened to us?
WOMAN:	Just trying to make ends meet . . .
MAN:	Just trying to get the kids through school . . .
WOMAN:	Maybe it's time we just tried to be married.
MAN:	Isn't that what we're doing?
WOMAN:	I don't know. I never see you anymore.
MAN:	Oh, we see each other—as one is coming in the door and the other is walking out of it.
WOMAN:	Somehow, I didn't picture marriage to be like this.
MAN:	Are you unhappy?
WOMAN:	Yes. (*pause*) But, not with you, I don't think. I'm just too tired to tell.
MAN:	We need time.
WOMAN:	We need time together.
MAN:	(*pauses, thinking*) How about tonight? Let's . . . (*whispers in her ear*).
WOMAN:	Honey, we can't do that! Not tonight.
MAN:	Why not?
WOMAN:	Well, Chris has practice, and I have to go out to—
MAN:	(*putting his finger over her lips*) I know. There's a million things going on, but not tonight. Let's make tonight for us.
WOMAN:	I can't believe you're saying this. Can we make this a habit?
MAN:	I don't see why not.
WOMAN:	With our schedules?
MAN:	Priorities.
WOMAN:	I love you.
MAN:	And I love you.

Scene 11 (at home)

MAN: Don't forget to go by the cleaners.
WOMAN: Don't forget to pick up Chris after practice and grab supper for you and the kids. I have a late choir rehearsal.
MAN: I hope you sing well.
WOMAN: Thanks.
MAN: I have to leave extra early in the morning—I'm having a breakfast meeting with a client.
WOMAN: Are we still having lunch together at that new garden place?
MAN: I wouldn't miss it.
WOMAN: Jamie's sick, stop by the drug store on your way home to pick up her prescription.
MAN: OK. I'll be late tonight. I've got a last minute meeting and some final paper...Hey, why don't you get a baby-sitter, come pick me up at the office around 6:45, and let's go to the mall?
WOMAN: Are you feeling all right?
MAN: We'll just walk around and be together.
WOMAN: Sounds great. There's a documentary on TV tomorrow night we have to watch for school.
MAN: I'll pick up some popcorn on the way home and we'll make it a family time.
WOMAN: (*pause*) Thank you.
MAN: Thank you for marrying me.

Opportunities for small group discussion

1. What are some of the culprits robbing you of your time and energy? Can you eliminate any of these culprits? Or work around them?
2. What are some things you wish you had time to do with your spouse? How can you make those a reality?
3. What can you do creatively *together* to accomplish your everyday tasks?

Resources for further reading

Arp, Dave and Claudia. *60 One-Minute Marriage-Builders.* Brentwood, Tenn.: Wolgemuth and Hyatt, Publishers, 1989.

Clark, Chap and Dee. *Let Me Ask You This.* Colorado Springs, Colo.: NavPress, 1991.

Our Night Out

Ah, the best laid plans . . . . We've all experienced times of setting aside everything to have some focused time together and nothing goes right. Sometimes you end up more upset with each other than when you began.

Marriage and intimacy is a dance involving an intricate set of steps: drawing close, retreating across the room, and then drawing close again in an effort to connect. A dance instructor told us that once you learn the steps, the goal is not to look at your feet but to look into your partner's eyes. But you still may step on each other's toes.

Production Notes

Theme: Marital dating, being together
Target Audience: Married adults
Degree of Difficulty: 4 (fun, witty dialogue)
Running Time: 3–4 minutes
Characters: DANIEL, husband and father
MEG, wife and mother
Setting: Their bedroom
Props: 2 chairs
General Notes: Treat this sketch as a dance. Have fun. This is a fairly typical marriage scene, which is where the initial humor is. But the creativity you bring to its staging can bring a deeper meaning to it. Have movement, and give it rhythm.

DANIEL:	It sure was good of your mom to drop in on us and give us a night out.
MEG:	Without the kids.
DANIEL:	I wonder what made your mother want to do that?
MEG:	I think it was something she saw on television the other night.
DANIEL:	Remind me to make sure she finds more time to watch television.
MEG:	A night out.

MARRIAGE

DANIEL: (*embraces her*) You and me.
MEG: Me and you.
DANIEL: Together. (*sighs*)
MEG: A whole night, just to ourselves.
DANIEL: What do you want to do?
MEG: I don't know. What do you want to do?
DANIEL: It doesn't matter. Whatever you want to do will be great.
MEG: No, Honey, you've been working hard all week long, so let's do what you want to do.
DANIEL: But Babe, you spend your every moment with the kids, and I go out all the time with clients, so let's do something special for you.
MEG: You go out all the time with clients?
DANIEL: Well, yeah—I mean, not all the time—just for lunch, every now and then.
MEG: OK, then we can do what I want.
DANIEL: (*romantically*) What do you want to do?
MEG: (*pouts*) I don't know.
DANIEL: (*sighs*) How about we go to a nice restaurant?
MEG: You do that all the time.
DANIEL: But not with you.
MEG: I want to do something different.
DANIEL: Like what?
MEG: I don't know. If we were going to go to a restaurant, where would we go?
DANIEL: Uhm, we could go to Fiddler's or Chez Pierre's.
MEG: No.
DANIEL: Just get dressed and we'll decide on the way.
MEG: But I can't get dressed until I know where we are going.
DANIEL: Wear that brown thing. It looks good on you.
MEG: Could you be a little more specific?
DANIEL: The, uhm, corduroy skirt thing.
MEG: I wore that to church on Sunday.
DANIEL: Well, we're not going to church.
MEG: That narrows it down. But we might run into someone from church.
DANIEL: No chance. They don't know where we're going, either. Just put on something nice.
MEG: What kind of nice?
DANIEL: Huh?
MEG: I mean, do I wear something nice like casual-nice, or nice like seminice, or nice like *nice?*
DANIEL: I don't know.
MEG: Then I don't know what to wear. Are you wearing what you have on?
DANIEL: Can I?
MEG: It depends on where we are going.

DANIEL:	Well, where do you want to go?
MEG:	I don't think I care anymore. Is there somewhere you want to go?
DANIEL:	Honey, this night is for you....
MEG:	The mall.
DANIEL:	What about it?
MEG:	Let's go to the mall. I've been needing to look for a dress.
DANIEL:	Oh, Honey....
MEG:	What's the matter? You don't want to go to the mall? You said all this time that it was my night out and—
DANIEL:	Fine, I'll go to the mall. That'll be fine.
MEG:	Are you saying, "That'll be fine," but in your heart you're really saying, "I'd rather get hit by a truck than go to the mall"?
DANIEL:	Honestly?
MEG:	Honey!
DANIEL:	Well, you asked me!
MEG:	Then I don't want to go to the mall.
DANIEL:	Why not?
MEG:	Because your heart's not in it.
DANIEL:	My heart is never in the mall. It's my money that's in the mall.
MEG:	Let's think of something else.
DANIEL:	We're running out of time.
MEG:	I just don't know. I really want to do something different.
DANIEL:	Different is a safari ride through the African Serengeti Plain—and it is too late for reservations. (*chuckles*)
MEG:	Sweetheart . . . don't make fun of me.
DANIEL:	Seriously, Meg, you need to decide.
MEG:	I always have to decide. It's always my responsibility to make the decisions about where we go, what we have for dinner, what the kids wear, what you wear. Can't you ever make a decision? If it's my night out, maybe what I want is for you to make the decision.
DANIEL:	Fine. Let's go dancing at Antonio's.
MEG:	No, I'm not in the mood.
DANIEL:	How have we gone from a free night all to ourselves to the need for marriage counseling?
MEG:	You're right, I'm sorry. I'm just in one of those moods. I don't know what I want to do, and I feel all this pressure. I'm just . . .
DANIEL:	Tired? (*MEG nods.*) I'm tired too. We've been going full steam for a couple of weeks now. Why don't we just stay home tonight?
MEG:	And miss the fun of deciding where we want to go?
DANIEL:	It would be something different. I have it! I am making a decision.
MEG:	What?

DANIEL:	Let's send your mom and the kids out! She said she'd baby-sit—we didn't say where.
MEG:	Where are they gonna go?
DANIEL:	Let them decide! We'll grab a video, stick some popcorn in the microwave, put our feet up on the coffee table, light some candles, and enjoy some peace and quiet in our own home.
MEG:	I guess I won't have to worry about what to wear.
DANIEL:	I'll go get rid of everyone, and we can enjoy our night out!

Opportunities for small group discussion

1. What are some of your near "date night" disasters? How were they resolved?
2. What are some of your expectations for a date night?

Resources for further reading

Bundschuh, Rick, and Dave Gilbert. *Dating Your Mate.* Eugene, Ore.: Harvest House Publishers, 1987.

Lerner, Harriet Goldhor. *The Dance of Intimacy.* New York: Harper and Row, 1989.

We Are So Different

When Nicole and I first started dating, our similarities attracted us to each other. Yet through the course of our marriage, we have discovered that we are very different. So much so that there are times of extreme hair pulling. But a good friend reminded us that our differences are the doorway to intimacy and wholeness. That gives us hope.

Production Notes

Theme: Differences, honoring each other, mutual submission
Target Audience: Married adults
Degree of Difficulty: 7 (Pacing is important. Let it move quickly at some points, breathe at others.)
Running Time: 9 minutes
Characters: WOMAN, newly married wife
MAN, newly married husband
Setting: 12 scenes of various settings
Props: Coffee table
Chair
Television remote control
Department store shopping bags
Tool box, shiny tools, and leather gloves that have been washed in the dishwasher
General Notes: The setting is very simple. Everything can be played downstage, with the chair and coffee table (a piano bench works just as well) slightly upstage and center. For scene 7, we stood upright and acted as if tugging at the covers of the bed.

Have fun with this piece and bring plenty of energy. For us, the sketch has a very light and humorous feel because we want to point out that differences are good. They are there, they can cause conflict, and that is not necessarily a bad thing. Keeping it light helps the audience to receive and accept that truth.

Marriage

Scene 1 (*the living room, both are on the phone, backs to each other*)

WOMAN: Hello, Mom?
MAN: Hello, Dad?
WOMAN: He proposed!
MAN: She accepted!
TOGETHER: Isn't that wonderful?
WOMAN: He's the strong, silent type.
MAN: She's so spontaneous and fun loving.
WOMAN: He has a plan for everything.
MAN: Carefree as the wind.
WOMAN: Reliable as the day is long.
TOGETHER: We are so different. (*look over shoulders at each other*) I love that!
MAN: She loves movies, animals, and shopping!
WOMAN: He's crazy about football and tools, and he has a really big family!
TOGETHER: We're going to be so happy together. (*look at each other very gushy-like and overly loving*)

Scene 2 (*their living room*)

WOMAN: If we left now, we could catch a four o'clock movie! What do you say?
MAN: (*in a chair, watching television*) Honey, the game is still on. Besides, all my family's coming over, remember?
WOMAN: I guess I forgot. Don't put your feet on the coffee table. Who's coming over? Your mom?
MAN: (*takes feet off coffee table, attention is on the television*) No, everybody! Mom, Dad, Billy, James, Uncle Frank, Aunt Betty, Carla, Grandma, and all the kids. We do everything together. I invited them over to watch the game. They'll be here around five.
WOMAN: Oh. But won't the game be over by then?
MAN: No, there's another one on after this. We'll have a barbecue at halftime and then dessert before the third game.
WOMAN: You've got a plan for this?
MAN: Of course. We've got football 'til midnight! (*puts his feet back on the coffee table*)
WOMAN: Well, what am I supposed to do?
MAN: (*shrugs, cheers the game*)
WOMAN: Charge! (*pulls out a credit card*) See ya later.

Scene 3 (*their living room*)

WOMAN: (*enters with full shopping bags*)
MAN: (*waking up, looks at watch*) It's midnight! Where have you been?
WOMAN: Shopping.
MAN: Shopping? I thought the stores closed at ten.
WOMAN: I had to go by the grocery store.
MAN: The grocery store?
WOMAN: The grocery store.
MAN: Why did you go by the grocery store?
WOMAN: Dog food.
MAN: Dog food?
WOMAN: Dog food.
MAN: We don't have a dog.
WOMAN: (*pause*) We do now.
MAN: (*shocked*) You bought a dog?
WOMAN: (*grabbing his hand, leading him off*) C'mon, help me bring in all the other stuff I bought.
MAN: You bought a dog?
WOMAN: (*excited*) I want you to meet Mammoth!
MAN: (*mouthing*) Mammoth?
WOMAN: He's got huge paws.
MAN: Paws?
WOMAN: Aren't you surprised?
MAN: *Surprised* would be accurate.

Scene 4 (*their kitchen*)

WOMAN: Surprise! (*She opens his tool box.*)
MAN: (*looking around*) What? What? What did you do?
WOMAN: I ran all your tools through the dishwasher.
MAN: (*notices toolbox*) Wha...Wha... Oh Honey!
WOMAN: They look great, huh?
MAN: Oh Honey.
WOMAN: I bet you didn't know they could clean up like that.
MAN: Yeah, especially the leather stuff. (*grabs a shriveled leather glove*)
WOMAN: I did good, huh?
MAN: Uhh, yeah, you did great. (*clutches tool box to his chest*) You did great.

Scene 5 (*their living room, both on the phone*)

MAN: She ran all my tools through the pot scrubber cycle in the dishwasher! Don't tell Uncle Frank. Oh, I'll never hear the end of this.

MARRIAGE

WOMAN: He hates the new dog! It doesn't fit in our budget. He's so practical, except when it comes to his family.
MAN: She bought eighty dollars worth of chew toys! She's pretty impulsive.
TOGETHER: We are so different. It's, um, challenging.
MAN: Tell Grandma thanks for the meatloaf.

Scene 6 (*their living room*)

WOMAN: Can I talk to you for a minute?
MAN: (*preoccupied with the television*) Uh-huh.
WOMAN: Can you turn the game off?
MAN: Honey! OK, I'll mute it.
WOMAN: (*walks around to stand in between MAN and television*) I want to talk more.
MAN: I think you talk enough.
WOMAN: That's not what I meant.
MAN: (*still preoccupied with the television, looking around her at it*) Oh.
WOMAN: I want us to talk more.
MAN: (*watching the game*) OK.
WOMAN: (*silence, waiting on him; takes remote control away from him*)
MAN: Hey! What do you want to talk about?
WOMAN: Never mind. It's not that important.

Scene 7 (*their bedroom*)

(*She is in bed; he enters and gets in bed.*)

MAN: Honey, wake up. We need a plan. Ooh, we need a plan.
WOMAN: No more barbecue at halftime.
MAN: No, I'm talking about the kids' education.
WOMAN: I think kindergarten is a great plan.
MAN: I'm talking about college.
WOMAN: I don't think they're ready.
MAN: Honey, wake up, this is the future. How are we going to pay for it?
WOMAN: Honey, this is the present—it's two-thirty in the morning. I don't care!
MAN: But this is critical.
WOMAN: I don't care. Wake me up when they're in high school.

Scene 8 (*At a party*)

WOMAN: High school? You knew him in high school?
MAN: Yes, now let's go.
WOMAN: We just got here.
MAN: No, we've been here for forty-five minutes. We put in an appearance, we talked to my boss, now I'm ready to go.

WOMAN:	You are no fun.
MAN:	This is not fun to me.
WOMAN:	You know I love parties. Let's dance.
MAN:	I don't want to dance.
WOMAN:	Let's talk to people.
MAN:	I don't want to talk to people. I hate people.
WOMAN:	Look, there are the Murphys. Smile!
MAN:	I don't want to smile. I want to go home. (*smiles weakly*) I feel sick.
WOMAN:	Look, there are the Purcells. Let's go talk to them. We've been wanting to meet them.
MAN:	I don't want to talk to the Purcells. (*She is pushing him to the Purcells.*) I don't know the Purcells.
TOGETHER:	Hi! Nice to see you.

Scene 9 (*their living room, both on the phone*)

WOMAN:	He wanted to leave the minute we got there!
MAN:	Four hours, Billy. We were there for four hours. I got desperate. I had to do something.
WOMAN:	He walked over to the refreshment table . . .
MAN:	I didn't know I could still do this.
WOMAN:	. . . and started making throwing up sounds over the punch bowl.
MAN:	It was so funny. I hadn't done that since high school.
WOMAN:	I was not laughing.
MAN:	Well, I got what I wanted. I mean, I got to go home. And, you know, she calls me stiff. Sometimes I think she is so flexible she could—
WOMAN:	make a gymnast look stiff. That's what he said to me. He cannot communicate.
MAN:	She won't shut up.
TOGETHER:	We are so different!
WOMAN:	And he's driving me crazy!

Scene 10 (*their living room*)

MAN:	Give me the credit card!
WOMAN:	No!
MAN:	Then take all the patio furniture back!
WOMAN:	No!
MAN:	OK, fine. (*looking around*) I can get two hundred dollars cash for that dog tomorrow.
WOMAN:	Fine! If the patio furniture goes back, I'll send the TV and the coffee table back with it!
MAN:	Fine! That means the VCR and the movies go back too!

MARRIAGE

WOMAN:	Fine! Maybe that will keep your family away for awhile!
MAN:	Well, if it doesn't, you can always run them all through the dishwasher!
WOMAN:	And then, after the rinse cycle, you can plan their lives to death!
TOGETHER:	We are so different!
WOMAN:	You drive me nuts! I've never met anyone more structured and rigid.
MAN:	You are so impulsive! It's irresponsible.
WOMAN:	You used to call me spontaneous and carefree. You said you loved that about me.
MAN:	Yeah?
WOMAN:	Yeah!
MAN:	Yeah, well, I lied!

Scene 11 (*their living room, both on the phone*)

WOMAN:	(*crying*) And then he said that he lied about the part that he loved me when I was spontaneous and carefree.
MAN:	I don't know why I said it, Grandma . . . Is Dad there?
WOMAN:	(*crying*) I don't know what we ever had in common, Mom.
MAN:	Of course we still love each other, Mom. It's just that . . . Is Dad there?
WOMAN:	Well, that's true. I guess I hadn't thought about it like that.
MAN:	You're right, Uncle Frank. I hadn't thought about it like that. Yeah, is Dad there? (*gets angry*) Yes, my tools are still shiny. Stop laughing, Uncle Frank! Get my father!
WOMAN:	So why does he drive me so crazy, Mom. Because I do? Really?
MAN:	You're right, Dad. I do.

Scene 12 (*their living room*)

MAN:	Sorry for what I said.
WOMAN:	Me too.
MAN:	You need to be spontaneous and fun loving. Grandma said so.
WOMAN:	And I know you need your structure. I may not like it, but I know you need it.
MAN:	Yeah.
WOMAN:	Here's the credit card. (*hands MAN the credit card*) I'm sorry about the patio furniture.
MAN:	(*takes card from WOMAN*) That's OK, but four umbrellas?
WOMAN:	I couldn't decide.
MAN:	(*smiles, handing credit card back to WOMAN*) Without you, my life would be boring, and I would be alone.
WOMAN:	(*taking card from MAN*) Boring? Maybe. Alone, with your family? I don't think so.

MAN:	We're different.
WOMAN:	We are different.
TOGETHER:	We are so different.
MAN:	But I love you. And I'm not going anywhere.
WOMAN:	Well, then, I guess we just found the one thing we're the same in. (*MAN and WOMAN hug.*)

Opportunities for small group discussion

1. What are some of the differences you have noticed in your marriage relationship? How do you feel about those differences?
2. What habits have you carried over from your family of origin? Are they a strength or an irritant to your mate? How can they be viewed as a strength?
3. What can your partner do that you cannot? How is that good? Where do you complete each other?

Resources for further reading

Kroeger, Otto, and Janet Thuesen. *Type Talk.* New York: Bantam Doubleday Dell Publishing Group, 1988.

Smalley, Gary, and John Trent. *The Two Sides of Love.* Pomona, Calif.: Focus on the Family Publishing, 1990.

Scripts

It was a moment of great revelation. Nicole and I had just finished another one of our "doozies." We had withdrawn to our respective corners and were licking our wounds. And then she asked the question, "Why do we always fight this same fight?" It stunned me. She was right. The argument had begun over a disagreement about something and tumbled right down to the same old "You always, I never, you are, I'm not . . ." fight.

Something in the disagreement touched a nerve in us and caused us to throw up our defenses. We felt like a defective part of our character had been exposed. We began the banter of "It's not my fault—it's yours . . . I'm not a bad person—and you can be worse." That pattern of behavior, creating walls with each other, is the heart of "Scripts."

Production Notes

Theme: Communication, intimacy, the ability to change
Target Audience: Married adults
Degree of Difficulty: 6 (see general notes)
Running Time: 7 minutes
Characters: BRIAN, husband, middle-aged
                   CATHERINE, wife, middle-aged
Setting: A meeting room; various locations within their household
Props: 2 scripts of two or three pages each
                   Chair
General Notes: Enjoy the comedy while maintaining the integrity of the situation. The transitions between the meeting room and the replay of the scripts need to be sharp and clean.

(*BRIAN and CATHERINE are standing centerstage, holding hands, very nervous. A chair is behind them.*)
CATHERINE: Hi, we're the Randolphs. And we got scripts.

BRIAN: My name is Brian, and this is my wife Catherine. We've known for quite some time that we had scripts; we just didn't want to talk about it. We were scared.

CATHERINE: The first time we ever told our story was a couple of months ago. We were standing in front of our support group—you know, for other couples who have scripts. I told 'em it all started one night, a year or so ago, when we were fighting. . . .

(*BRIAN and CATHERINE step upstage to either side of the chair. Begin "Kids Script."*)

CATHERINE: Why do you speak to him like that?
BRIAN: Like what?
CATHERINE: Like he can't do anything right.
BRIAN: I didn't speak to him like that.
CATHERINE: You don't know how you come across.
BRIAN: And I guess you are going to tell me how I come across.
CATHERINE: You should just be nicer to him.
BRIAN: Like you are?
CATHERINE: I didn't say that.
BRIAN: You might as well have. I don't want to treat him like you treat him. I'm his father; you're his mother.
CATHERINE: He needs more from you.
BRIAN: When did you become such a parenting expert?
CATHERINE: When you became such a rotten parent.

(*End "Kids Script."*)

BRIAN: And then it hit me. We'd had this argument before. (*BRIAN and CATHERINE join hands and move back downstage center.*) We both stood there staring at each other with that overwhelming sense of déjà vu, and I said, "Catherine, we've fought this fight before."

CATHERINE: And I said, "Brian, we've fought this fight a hundred times before." You see, that's the "aha!" moment for people who have scripts. If you don't have that We've-been-here-before moment, you either don't have scripts or you still don't know that you have scripts.

BRIAN: Over the next few months, we noticed that five scripts began to surface in our marriage.

CATHERINE: Five scripts are pretty bad. But we ain't as bad as that one couple. Remember them? They had eighteen different scripts in their marriage. They told their story last week.

BRIAN: Yeah, it took a long time too. Now, "scripts" are those little plays that we use in our marriages or relationships when we're talking to each other without really listening or paying attention. Or when we're defending our own points of view and don't really know why. You know, like the Garbage Script.

CATHERINE:	Yeah, we had the Kids Script, the Garbage Script, the Sex Script, the Silent Script, and the Money Script. We knew we had them; we just didn't know what to do about them.
BRIAN:	I actually tried to deny that we even had scripts. I mean, when we'd argue, we'd try not to use our scripts. We'd even argue about something completely different so we didn't come back to our scripts.
CATHERINE:	But we always came back to them. The more we tried not to use them, the more they flowed right out of our mouths. We were fighting like cats and dogs every day. There was hardly anything either of us could say that didn't trigger one of our scripts.

(*BRIAN moves to the chair, sits in it, and acts as if watching television. CATHERINE moves stage left as if in the kitchen. Begin "Garbage Script."*)

CATHERINE:	Brian, I need you to take the garbage out.
BRIAN:	(*pauses, lost in the television*) OK, Hon, in a minute.
CATHERINE:	(*moves to stand behind him*) You always say that and then you never do it. Now, get up and go do it. (*pushes him out of the chair*)
BRIAN:	You never give me enough time.
CATHERINE:	Was last week enough time?
BRIAN:	You always exaggerate. (*sits back in chair*)
CATHERINE:	You never do what I ask you to do.
BRIAN:	'Cause you always go on and do it yourself.
CATHERINE:	'Cause you never do anything around here.
BRIAN:	'Cause you're always naggin' and gripin'.
CATHERINE:	'Cause you never get up from the TV.
BRIAN:	'Cause you always want me to do something.
CATHERINE:	'Cause you never spend any time with me.

(*End "Garbage Script."*)

BRIAN:	(*moving back to downstage center*) Then one day—I still can't believe it when I think about it—Catherine, she, uh . . . (*looks at CATHERINE, who is still back at the chair*) Come here, Baby. . . . (*takes CATHERINE'S hand and pulls her to him*) She says to me, "Brian, I can't live like this anymore." We were stuck, and I knew it, but I didn't know what to do about it. So I did nothing.
CATHERINE:	Brian's right. I felt like I was drowning, and he was just watching me. I knew we needed help, I knew we needed to change, but I was afraid that he didn't want to change anything.
BRIAN:	I wanted to change. I just thought she was looking to me to be the one to change things. I didn't know where to start. I was scared to death too. I was.
CATHERINE:	I guess at this point we can share with them the "biggie."
BRIAN:	(*He sucks in his breath and starts to protest. CATHERINE reassures him. Brian lets out a long, low whistle.*)

Marriage

(*Begin "Sex Script." BRIAN crosses in front of CATHERINE to downstage left; CATHERINE moves to downstage right.*)

BRIAN: Why not?
CATHERINE: Because I'm not "in the mood."
BRIAN: (*crossing to her*) You're never in the mood.
CATHERINE: You're never *not* in the mood. I'm tired and I don't want to.
BRIAN: (*turns away from her, pouting*) Fine.
CATHERINE: Now you're mad.
BRIAN: No, I'm not.
CATHERINE: Yes, you are.
BRIAN: Well, how long has it been?
CATHERINE: I don't know.
BRIAN: (*moves to her, obviously frustrated*) Three weeks, four days, five hours, and thirteen minutes.
CATHERINE: Good grief.
BRIAN: See, you don't know. What does that say about you?
CATHERINE: That I'm not preoccupied.
BRIAN: Preoccupied! You're not even postoccupied. You're so unoccupied, it's not even funny.
CATHERINE: Well, I have a lot to do.
BRIAN: Like I don't?
CATHERINE: I just don't have time!
BRIAN: Once a month? You wash the dog more than that.
CATHERINE: I enjoy washing the dog.
BRIAN: (*stunned*) Ohhhhh! Ohhhh!
CATHERINE: I was making a joke.
BRIAN: (*angry*) There's a little bit of truth in every joke we tell.
CATHERINE: Even the jokes you make about my weight?
BRIAN: (*stunned again*) No.
CATHERINE: See there, you think I'm fat?
BRIAN: Honey, I'm fat too.
CATHERINE: Darn right you are—but it doesn't seem to bother you. And you don't see me making jokes about it. Just leave me alone. I'm tired and I said no!

(*End of "Sex Script."*)

BRIAN: Usually that led us right into the Silent Script.

(*BRIAN and CATHERINE begin "Silent Script," go through a series of sighs, visual chases, and head turns, never making direct eye contact.*)

CATHERINE: Then it was just a matter of time before we got to the Money Script.

(*BRIAN and CATHERINE move upstage to either side of the chair. Begin "Money Script."*)

BRIAN: We just don't have it.
CATHERINE: Yes, we do.

BRIAN:	Why is there always something? Why do you always want more?
CATHERINE:	What, more toilet paper? More shoes for the kids? You're right, I'm so extravagant.
BRIAN:	Why can't I say no to you?
CATHERINE:	You can. You're doing it right now. You're absolutely great at it!
BRIAN:	You know you'd spend every last dime we had.
CATHERINE:	Wrong! I could never pry it out of your clenched fist!

(*End "Money Script." BRIAN and CATHERINE move together to down center.*)

BRIAN:	Well, that's our five scripts: the Kids Script, the Garbage Script, the Sex Script, the Silent Script, and the Money Script. We stand before you tonight and confess our desire that our scripts be torn up and thrown into the trash can!
CATHERINE:	We want to deal with our stuff right when it comes up. We don't want the scripts that our parents wrote, or that the TV wrote, to keep playing out in our marriage. And most of all, we want to stop writing scripts ourselves.
BRIAN:	People can change.
CATHERINE:	Yes, they can.
BRIAN:	And God is merciful enough to show us how.
CATHERINE:	Yes, he is.
BRIAN:	Apart from his love and grace, which has found us, we'd stay stuck using our scripts and, over time, our marriage would just become so well rehearsed that our souls would die while we continued repeating lines like broken records.
CATHERINE:	We're hoping and praying for something more than that.
BRIAN:	We're hoping and praying for a lot more than that.

(*Tear up scripts together and fling them into the air.*)

Opportunities for small group discussion

1. What are some other topics that become scripts?
2. How can we hold ourselves accountable to facing the truth and not depending on scripts in our communication with our spouses?

Resources for further reading

Crabb, Larry. *Inside Out.* Colorado Springs, Colo.: NavPress, 1988.

Markman, Howard, Scott Stanley, and Susan Blumberg. *Fighting for Your Marriage.* San Francisco: Jossey-Bass Publishers, 1994.

Smalley, Gary. *If Only He Knew.* Grand Rapids, Mich.: Zondervan Publishing House, 1979.

———. *For Better or Best.* Grand Rapids, Mich.: Zondervan Publishing House, 1979.

The Ledger People

The eighth definition of *love* in Webster's dictionary reads: "a score of zero, as in the game of tennis." In tennis or in God's kingdom, the truth is, real love does not keep score. Yet often, our human love, especially in this culture of "winning is everything," keeps score constantly. It is always judging, evaluating, grading, and comparing. And that kind of love proves deadly for marriages and families.

"The Ledger People" exposes this myth and reveals that our only hope is forgiveness: a conscious decision to lay down our right for retribution and to let the other person go free; to grant release; to put down the ledgers.

Real love does not keep score. We are never more like God than when we lay down our score cards and forgive.

Production Notes

Theme: Love, grace, forgiveness
Target Audience: Adults
Degree of Difficulty: 7 (involves manipulation of ledger props; contains strong emotional content)
Running Time: 8 minutes
Characters: JIM, husband, middle-aged
SALLY, wife, middle-aged
Setting: The kitchen of their home
Props: 2 ledgers
2 pens
Newspaper
Sales receipts
Apron for SALLY with big pocket to keep her ledger
General Notes: In the opening part of the sketch, the ease and "normalness" of the way JIM and SALLY live with their ledgers is crucial. It must look as though they have a great system. The writing and recording in their ledgers must be flawless and look as though it is no trouble. Their ledgers are extensions of their arms.

Pay attention to JIM's turning point in the sketch. His realization of their marriage pattern and of the way they live remains the powerful climax of this piece. It must be strong, passionate, and believable.

The rest of the sketch focuses on the threat of SALLY's comfortable system being taken away from her, and this exposes the real fears she has about her marriage.

(*JIM comes in the kitchen door from work with his newspaper and ledger tucked underneath his arm. SALLY has on her apron with her ledger tucked in the front pocket. Until the sketch turns to how badly JIM needs points, SALLY busies herself with fixing dinner.*)

JIM: Hello, Sweetheart.

SALLY: Hi, Honey. You're home early.

JIM: Third time this week.

SALLY: I guess you expect me to write that down.

JIM: When you get a chance, it would be nice.

SALLY: How was work?

JIM: Not good. You know that proposal I've been working on the past couple of weeks?

SALLY: (*nodding*) Uh-huh.

JIM: Well, I finished it and submitted it to Mike and Robert. As I was leaving the office, I overheard them talking about it, and it wasn't too kindly. I went to write it down in my ledger, and I realized that it was the third negative comment they've made about my performance THIS WEEK! They're really coming up short here lately.

SALLY: (*writing in her ledger*) I'm sorry, Honey. I know how you feel. My mother has three pages of minuses, and I'm just not sure how to tell her.

JIM: I'll tell her.

SALLY: That's OK.

JIM: (*shrugs, walks up behind her*) What's for dinner?

SALLY: Lasagna. And salad.

JIM: Ooh, my favorite. All right, I'll write it down. Somehow you always know. (*He opens the ledger to record "+2" for the lasagna. He notices a string of pluses.*) Whoa! Look at this. Ten pluses in a row for you.

SALLY: I've been trying.

JIM: That's quite a turnaround from last weekend.

SALLY: Honey, I said I was sorry.

JIM: Yeah, well, the proof is in the ledger. (*records the pluses*) That was some shopping spree last weekend.

SALLY:	Strawberry shortcake for dessert.
JIM:	(*looking up from ledger*) Are you planning another purchase? OK, one more point—
SALLY:	One? I should get two points for that.
JIM:	Two? Why two?
SALLY:	One for the strawberries and one for the shortcake.
JIM:	Store-bought shortcake?
SALLY:	Nope.
JIM:	Frozen strawberries?
SALLY:	Nope.
JIM:	OK, two points. (*records another "+2" in his ledger*)
SALLY:	Thanks.
JIM:	Where are the kids?
SALLY:	Jenny's gone to Elizabeth's. Elizabeth was here yesterday, so it's OK, and Billy's in his room.
JIM:	I thought Billy had football practice.
SALLY:	He did, but I kept him home. Today is the third day in a row that he forgot his social studies homework from school, and it's the third week in a row that his balance has fallen below acceptable levels.
JIM:	That is not good.
SALLY:	So he is in his room thinking.
JIM:	Billy? Hmm.
SALLY:	Oh, Bob called. He wants to borrow your mower.
JIM:	Oh, not again. He kept it four days last time.
SALLY:	You told him it was OK.
JIM:	Yeah, but I didn't mean it. You know I'll have to think of something I can borrow of his.
SALLY:	It's OK if it stays on the ledger awhile.
JIM:	That's true! It's not like I borrowed first. That's excellent. I'll give you another point for that. (*crosses to table to put his paper down*)
SALLY:	Thanks.
JIM:	Wait a minute, (*picks up receipt*) what's this receipt over here on the table?
SALLY:	A gift I bought for Susan.
JIM:	What occasion?
SALLY:	She bought me something.
JIM:	Really?
SALLY:	Yeah, she just showed up with a little gift basket yesterday around lunch time.
JIM:	Was she one down?
SALLY:	(*defensively*) Not by my records.
JIM:	So, out of the blue, she just brought a gift?

SALLY:	Yep.
JIM:	(*He whistles softly.*)
SALLY:	I was really embarrassed. I don't know why she did that. So I picked her up a bath basket to balance out the ledger, so I can sleep tonight.
JIM:	Is that why you were tossing around last night? You know, you kept me up long enough to take away some of your points.
SALLY:	Wait a minute—(*they begin to speak on top of each other, very heatedly.*)
JIM:	Just kidding. It's just a joke—
SALLY:	That's not funny!
JIM:	It was just a joke. You know you had ten in a row—
SALLY:	That's not funny at all. You don't kid around with these things (*starts to remove her ledger from her apron*)
JIM:	Hey! Hey! I was only kidding! Don't take away any of my points!
SALLY:	I'm not taking away any of your points!
JIM:	Well, then take your hand off of it! (*SALLY withdraws her hand from her ledger like she is being held at gunpoint*) It was a joke!
SALLY:	I didn't know.
JIM:	I was kidding!
SALLY:	I didn't know!
JIM:	Well, learn! (*They both stare at each other as in a standoff. Both look away at the same time.*)
JIM:	(*calmer, but still mad*) What time is dinner?
SALLY:	Not for another thirty minutes.
JIM:	OK, I'm going to read the paper.
SALLY:	No points for that.
JIM:	That's OK, I enjoy it.
SALLY:	You'll get some points if you run.
JIM:	I don't enjoy that. Did you go to aerobics this morning?
SALLY:	No.
JIM:	I'll go read the paper.
SALLY:	But I did walk Jenny to the bus stop.
JIM:	Goodness. Do I really need the points?
SALLY:	Yep, you really need the points.
JIM:	Really?
SALLY:	Badly.
JIM:	Badly? How badly?
SALLY:	(*opening her ledger to get the exact count*) As of this afternoon, you make Billy look good.
JIM:	No way! I've been home early three times this week.
SALLY:	(*consulting the ledger*) But you worked late four times last week.
JIM:	You took away points for that? I was trying to get some overtime pay.
SALLY:	What do you mean by that?

JIM: Well, it's just that since you quit work, I've had to take up the slack around here.

SALLY: That was a mutually agreed upon decision. Did I lose points for that?

JIM: Just a few.

SALLY: You are so sneaky. Minus ten.

JIM: Minus ten! From what? You subtract my points like it was some kind of hobby! Ohhh, now. Don't you cry. Don't you dare start crying.

SALLY: (*between sobs*) Minus five more.

JIM: I did not make you cry. You started crying on your own free will. That's only two points.

SALLY: I can't stand you!

JIM: Ooh! Minus ten big ones!

SALLY: I said "can't stand." I did not say "hate."

JIM: But you meant "hate."

SALLY: But I said "can't stand." It doesn't matter what you mean; it only matters what you say.

JIM: Oh? Is that it? (*contemplates the new rule*) And compliments, they are one point each, is that right? (*drippingly sweet*) You look lovely tonight, Honey.

SALLY: Stop it.

JIM: And your hair . . . oh, your hair is beautiful. And kisses are two apiece, aren't they? (*kisses her*) I'm up to four. You better write it down.

SALLY: I'm not writing anything down.

JIM: But you have to! I'm getting my points—the old-fashioned way—I'm earning them!

SALLY: No, you're not being fair.

JIM: Fair? I spend my life being indebted to you, working my way back to the black! I don't have time to be fair!

SALLY: It's the only way to make sure everything stays fair. It's the only way to be sure you are doing for me as much as I do for you.

JIM: Well, what if I don't want to?

SALLY: (*pause*) Excuse me? (*She opens the ledger again.*)

JIM: What if I'm tired of keeping up with who is doing what for whom? What if I am sick of pluses, minuses and ledgers and points? (*pause, looks at ledger, then pleads*) What if I want to do something for you? No points involved. Just because I love you.

SALLY: (*She consults her ledger.*) I'd give you some bonus points for that.

JIM: Stop it! Don't you see? Sally, that's just it. We spend our lives making sure everything gets recorded in these books. (*looks at open ledger in his hands, closes it forcefully, and throws it on the table*) I'm closing my ledger for good.

SALLY: Wait Jim, you can't close your ledger. (*She goes and gets his ledger.*)

JIM: Just did.

SALLY: What about all my points?

Marriage

JIM: What about them? They don't matter to me.

SALLY: But they matter to me. What will I get for them?

JIM: Nothing. I love you. Isn't that enough?

SALLY: I don't know.

JIM: (*crosses to her*) So you love your point balance more than you love me?

SALLY: I didn't say that. It's just easier for you to close your ledger because you're behind, because you're losing.

JIM: (*pauses, looks around*) You're right, Sally. I am losing. I'm losing you; I'm losing the kids; I'm losing me.

SALLY: (*continues to stare at the ledger*) What are you going to do about all your minuses?

JIM: (*tenderly*) I could never turn them into pluses.

SALLY: But you could try.

JIM: There are not enough lifetimes. (*He reaches for the ledgers and pulls them to him. SALLY does not let go.*) I'll just have to ask for your forgiveness.

SALLY: Just like that? What about next time?

JIM: If the ledger is closed, where will you write it down?

SALLY: If the ledger is closed, how will you do what you're supposed to do around here?

JIM: And what am I supposed to do, Sally? Love you or keep score? If I'm trying to win, I can't love you. (*releases ledgers to SALLY*)

SALLY: But do you really want to love me? Or do you want to win?

JIM: I want to love you.

SALLY: For no points?

JIM: For no points.

SALLY: No bonuses?

JIM: No bonuses.

SALLY: For free?

JIM: For free.

SALLY: (*She crosses to the table. JIM remains downstage, looking away from her, concerned with what she will do. SALLY drops the ledgers on the table. JIM turns to her with the sound of the ledgers on the table. SALLY looks at him, holds her hands up in a gesture that shows she is no longer holding on. JIM extends his hand to her. She crosses to him and takes his hand. JIM smiles reassuringly. SALLY, unsure, returns a half smile. Lights dim with them holding hands, looking at each other.*)

Opportunities for small group discussion

1. Why is keeping score important to some people?
2. How do you feel when faced with the real possibility of losing?
3. What does being "one-up" do to your attitude toward other people?

4. Why doesn't Jim just simply walk away from the relationship when he is losing so much? What keeps some people from walking away, and what keeps others from staying?
5. How does one develop the attitude of laying down one's "life for his friends"? (John 15:13).

Resources for further reading

Allendar, Dan, and Tremper Longman. *Bold Love*. Colorado Springs, Colo.: NavPress, 1992.

Brown, Stephen. *When Being Good Isn't Good Enough*. Nashville: Thomas Nelson Publishers, 1990.

Johnson, Paul and Nicole. *Random Acts of Grace.* Nashville: Broadman and Holman, 1998.

One Flesh

Marriage is about growing together as individuals, working to complete each other in the way God intended. The giving of one's self is the integral component to this completion. It is not easy. In fact, it is quite painful at times. But a rich, deep, intimate marriage of many years provides the most convincing evidence and the most valid testimony that "the greatest of these is love" (1 Cor. 13:13).

For "One Flesh" we pulled together some of the scriptural references for marriage to point out the goal of oneness in marriage, and the foundation of love as sacrifice.

Production Notes

Theme: Love, marriage
Target Audience: Married adults
Degree of Difficulty: 6 (needs creative blocking and accurate timing)
Running Time: 5–6 minutes
Characters: MAN
                     WOMAN
Setting: General
Props: None
General Notes: This sketch requires creativity in its blocking to keep it interesting and lively. We have made a couple of notes to generate creative blocking ideas, though we urge you to come up with your own. Timing is also critical to keep the pace of the sketch moving.

    Try using an actual husband and wife for the two narrators. It will add an interesting dynamic to the presentation of the sketch, as well as making it more fun for the audience.

MAN: "The LORD God said,
TOGETHER: 'It is not good for the man to be alone. I will make a helper suitable for him.'

Marriage

MAN:	So the LORD God caused the man to fall into a deep sleep; *(nods off)*
WOMAN:	and while he was sleeping, he took one of the man's ribs and closed up the place with flesh. Then the LORD God made a woman from the rib he had taken out of the man." [Gen. 2:18, 21–22]
MAN:	*(awaking)* "This is it! You are bone of my bones, and flesh of my flesh; you shall be called
WOMAN:	'Woman,'
MAN:	for you were taken from my side." [Gen. 2:23, paraphrased]
WOMAN:	"For this reason a man will leave his father and mother
MAN:	and be united to his wife,
TOGETHER:	and they WILL become ONE flesh." [Gen. 2:24] *(lock hands to arm wrestle each line)*
WOMAN:	My flesh or yours?
MAN:	Do you ever think about divorce?
WOMAN:	Divorce? No. Murder? Yes.
MAN:	The Bible says, "Let the women keep silent . . . [and] subject themselves." [1 Cor. 14:34 NASB]
WOMAN:	The Bible also says, "Let the husband fulfill his duty to his wife." [1 Cor. 7:3 NASB]
MAN:	"The contentions of a wife are a constant dripping. . . ." Drip, drip, drip. [Prov. 27:15, paraphrased]
WOMAN:	"Don't deal treacherously with the wife of your youth." [Mal. 2:15, paraphrased]
MAN:	"Your husband is your Maker"! [Isa. 54:5 NASB]
WOMAN:	Yeah, you make her do this and you make her do that.
MAN:	You need a "gentle and quiet spirit"! [1 Pet. 3:4]
WOMAN:	Husband, provoke not your wife!
MAN:	"Submit to your husband"! [Eph. 5:22]
WOMAN:	"Love your wife"! [Eph. 5:33, paraphrased].
MAN:	"Better to live on a corner of the roof than share a house with a quarrelsome wife"! [Prov. 21:9; 25:24]
WOMAN:	"Husbands . . . live with your wives in an understanding way, as with a weaker vessel, . . . and grant her honor as a fellow-heir of the grace of life, so that your prayers may not be hindered"! [1 Pet. 3:7 NASB]
MAN:	*(stops wrestling)* And the two . . .
WOMAN:	*(reluctantly)* And the two . . .
MAN:	shall become?
WOMAN:	shall become . . .
MAN:	one flesh.
WOMAN:	One flesh.
TOGETHER:	"Submit to one another out of reverence for Christ." [Eph. 5:21]

MAN:	"Two are better than one, because they have a good return—"
WOMAN:	Do we file jointly?
MAN:	"for their work:
WOMAN:	If one falls down, his friend can help him up.
MAN:	But pity the [one] who falls and has no one to help [her] up!
WOMAN:	Also, if two lie down together,
MAN:	they will keep warm.
WOMAN:	But how can one keep warm alone?
MAN:	Though one may be overpowered,
WOMAN:	two can defend themselves.
TOGETHER:	*(MAN embraces WOMAN.)* A cord of three strands is not quickly broken." [Eccles. 4:9–12]
WOMAN:	I lovest thou.
MAN:	That's King James for "I love you."
WOMAN:	"And now [we] will show you the most excellent way.
MAN:	If I speak in the tongues of men and of angels, . . .
WOMAN:	If I have the gift of prophecy and can fathom all mysteries and all knowledge, . . ."
MAN:	If I corrected my wife with the wisdom of the ages . . .
WOMAN:	If I drove the carpool five times a week . . .
MAN:	"If I have a faith that can move mountains, . . .
WOMAN:	If I give all I possess to the poor
MAN:	and surrender my body to the flames, . . ."
WOMAN:	Or donated my organs to medicine . . .
MAN:	"But have not love, . . ."
WOMAN:	but have not love,
TOGETHER:	but have not love,
MAN:	I am nothing.
WOMAN:	"I gain nothing." [1 Cor. 13:1–3]
MAN:	"I may act kindly, correctly, justly toward my wife and yet withhold the giving of myself, which is love." [C. S. Lewis]
WOMAN:	"Love is patient,"
MAN:	It's OK, Honey, give it one more try.
WOMAN:	"love is kind."
MAN:	It's not my favorite, but it does look very nice on you.
WOMAN:	"It does not envy,"
MAN:	My wife is much better with the checkbook than I am.
WOMAN:	"it does not boast,"
MAN:	"it is not proud."
WOMAN:	I could never have done it without your help.
MAN:	"[Love] is not rude,"

MARRIAGE

WOMAN:	I'm sorry I always interrupt you.
MAN:	"[love] is not self-seeking,"
WOMAN:	No, I'd like to watch the ballgame.
MAN:	"[love] is not easily angered, it keeps no record of wrongs."
TOGETHER:	Love does not keep score.
MAN:	"Love does not delight in evil
WOMAN:	but rejoices with the truth.
MAN:	It always protects,
WOMAN:	always trusts,
MAN:	always hopes,
WOMAN:	always perseveres.
TOGETHER:	Love never fails." [1 Cor. 13:4–8]
MAN:	It never fails.
WOMAN:	Love never fails.
MAN:	Never will it fail.
WOMAN:	Love never fails.
TOGETHER:	For love comes from God.
WOMAN:	"Let us fix our eyes on Jesus, . . .
MAN:	So that [we] will not grow weary and lose heart." [Heb. 12:2–3]
WOMAN:	"Let us place our hope in the LORD,
MAN:	for he will renew our strength.
WOMAN:	And we will soar on wings like eagles." [Isa. 40:31, paraphrased]
TOGETHER:	One flesh!
WOMAN:	"And now these three remain: faith,"
MAN:	faith,
WOMAN:	"hope,"
MAN:	hope,
WOMAN:	"and love."
MAN:	love.
WOMAN:	"But the greatest of these"
MAN:	The greatest of all of these . . .
TOGETHER:	"is love." [1 Cor. 13:13]

Opportunities for small group discussion

1. What does it mean to submit to each other out of reverence to Christ?
2. What are ways that we give of ourselves? What does it mean for you to specifically give of yourself in the context of your marriage?
3. How do the "love is . . ." statements of 1 Corinthians 13 translate in your marriage?

Resources for further reading

Crabb, Larry. *The Marriage Builder.* Grand Rapids, Mich.: Zondervan Publishing House, 1982.
Andrews, Otis and Deigie. *Husbands and Wives, the Best of Friends.* Nashville: Lifeway Press, 1994.
Miller, Calvin. *If This Be Love.* San Francisco: Harper and Row, 1984.
Wangerin, Walter, Jr. *As for Me and My House.* Nashville: Thomas Nelson Publishers, 1990.

Hidden Anger

Anger is one of the major destroyers of marriages. Anger, as an emotion, signals that something is wrong and that appropriate action should be taken. Yet, often we react more to the anger than to the problem. We lash out with intention to harm emotionally, spiritually, and physically. We react in anger toward "the enemy," the one we believe, truthfully or not, is trying to harm us. "Hidden Anger" seeks to expose the real enemy of some people's hurting marriages and the damage it can cause.

Production Notes

Theme: Anger, forgiveness
Target Audience: Married adults
Degree of Difficulty: 10 (very emotional piece, character-driven)
Running Time: 11 minutes
Characters: RICHARD, husband, middle-aged
LAURA, wife, middle-aged
Setting: The living room of their home
Props: 2 chairs
Small table
Dish towel
Briefcase
Picture frame with photograph in it
General Notes: Spend time discussing the characters, who they are, how they got to this place, and how and why they feel the way they feel. The emotions are deep, and the trick is knowing which to bring to the surface, and when, without going "over the top." These people have so much pain they don't want their partner to see, and it comes out in the cutting words they use to inflict pain on each other. Take your time with it, let there be energy, but don't rush the scene, especially the last third of the piece. Devote much time in rehearsal on this one.

MARRIAGE

(RICHARD enters with briefcase and coat in hand. He walks by LAURA without saying anything. She just glares. He puts his briefcase and coat down, then loosens his tie.)

RICHARD: Are the kids in bed?
LAURA: Yeah, finally. I'm surprised you made it home so early.
RICHARD: It's 8:30.
LAURA: That's early for you.
RICHARD: Laura, there's something we need to talk about. (*pause*) I met with an attorney this afternoon . . .
LAURA: Don't do this, Richard.
RICHARD: Laura, this is not working.
LAURA: You make it sound so functional. Like a machine breaking down.
RICHARD: It has broken down.
LAURA: That's because you want a machine, not a marriage.
RICHARD: I want a relationship.
LAURA: Do you think you are the only one in this room who is unhappy? You're just the only one who is quitting.
RICHARD: Maybe I have the courage to know when to quit.
LAURA: That's not courage.
RICHARD: You don't know how hard you are to live with.
LAURA: And I'm married to Mr. Cakewalk?
RICHARD: I'm not saying that. We're just too different.
LAURA: Yeah, I want to work on this marriage and you don't. That's pretty different.
RICHARD: That's not true. I just don't know what else to do.
LAURA: So you quit. How original!
RICHARD: Laura, I'm sick of our constant bickering. I'm tired of your criticism and your worn out martyrdom. I want peace, and I need to get away from you to get it.
LAURA: You really think peace is a place, don't you?
RICHARD: Why do you think I work so much?
LAURA: Because you're not very good at what you do?
RICHARD: Stop insulting me! That's all you ever do!
LAURA: It helps pass the hours I'm alone.
RICHARD: I cannot talk to you.
LAURA: Why start now?
RICHARD: (*silence*)
LAURA: So you just run away?
RICHARD: (*silence*)
LAURA: I think this is a pattern for you.

RICHARD:	(*silence*)
LAURA:	After you divorce me, I'd get that looked at.
RICHARD:	(*unbelieving what he is hearing this time*) You are so mean.
LAURA:	Mean? You're leaving me and you call me "mean"?
RICHARD:	You don't see your part in any of this, do you? You can't say two words to me without criticizing me. You blow up at everything I do. You yell at me every day before breakfast. You've got a really big problem, Laura, and it didn't start with me!
LAURA:	I was just waiting for that to come up. Now blame me for everything you do wrong.
RICHARD:	You are an angry person, and you don't know how to receive love.
LAURA:	How can you receive something that's never been given?
RICHARD:	I will not stand here and let you say I have never loved you. I've loved you, but you won't let it in. I could do everything in the world for you, and it wouldn't be enough.
LAURA:	Maybe I don't want you to do everything in the world. Maybe I just want you to love me.
RICHARD:	I have loved you! I have loved you with all I am. I've given you all I've got, and yet you treat me like I abuse you. You are angry at the world, but you only take it out on me.
LAURA:	You haven't given me anything. You're gone all the time. You don't spend any time with me, or the kids. You ignore me, and now you're leaving me. How can you say this is my fault? How can you say—
RICHARD:	Ssh! Wait a minute.... (*RICHARD goes to the doorway to the hall and begins speaking to one of their children.*) Katy, what are you doing up?
LAURA:	Go back to bed, Katy.
RICHARD:	(*to LAURA*) Shhh. (*to Katy*) No, Honey, Mommy's not mad at you. She's a little upset with me, but everything's fine. Go back to bed, Sweetheart. You're scared? A big girl like you? What are you scared of? Diborse? Oh, divorce. Don't be scared, Katy.
LAURA:	I'm scared too, Katy....
RICHARD:	C'mon, back to bed. Where did you get this picture? Let's go put it back. (*RICHARD exits momentarily and then reenters the room carrying a picture in a frame. He sets the picture on the table.*) Katy was holding this.
LAURA:	I guess it means something to Katy.
RICHARD:	You know, Laura, you say you want to work on this marriage, but you take any opportunity to just twist the knife! That's why it'll never work between us. I'm going to bed.
LAURA:	Sleep well.
RICHARD:	I will. (*exits*)

LAURA:	(*looking at the picture*) Vacation 1979. Why would Katy pick this picture? I think we were actually happy then. (*She stares at the picture and then starts to put it back on the table.*) What happened to us, Richard? (*She stares intently at the picture.*) I still remember the huge fight we had....
LAURA:	(*speaking to the picture*) Five years together! I'm glad we're away.
RICHARD:	(*from off stage*) Me too. It's good to take a few days. I know you've needed it for awhile.
LAURA:	You know I've needed it for awhile—what do you mean by that?
RICHARD:	Just that you've seemed stressed, that's all.
LAURA:	I've seemed stressed? About what?
RICHARD:	I don't know. I was hoping we could talk about it.
LAURA:	There's nothing to talk about.
RICHARD:	(*pause*) Laura, have I done something wrong? Are you angry with me?
LAURA:	Why do you always want to know if I'm angry? I get angry when you ask me if I'm angry.
RICHARD:	OK, I'm sorry. I'll drop it. Let's go somewhere fun.
LAURA:	I don't want to go anywhere now.
RICHARD:	Laura, please!
LAURA:	I don't want to go anywhere with you. Just leave me alone. Just leave me alone....
LAURA:	Why do you always bring up my anger? Even back then you were doing it. What difference does it make? Maybe I have a lot to be angry about. You've always had it perfect, Richard. (*begins to take picture out of the frame*) What would you know about anger? You didn't lose your Dad when you were twelve. Do you know how hard that is? Both of your parents are still alive. They see and know our kids. You got to finish college, and I had to work. You have a degree, and I have nothing. Now you make all the money, and I have to stay home and feel worthless half the time. (*rips up picture*) Oh God, I am angry. And I'm angry at you too. Where have you been? Why are you letting my marriage fall apart? And why did you take my daddy? Please help me. What have I done? O God, help me.
RICHARD:	(*entering*) Laura, where is the aspirin?
LAURA:	It's under the sink in the bathroom cabinet. (*RICHARD starts to exit.*) Richard?
RICHARD:	What? (*turns toward her, but doesn't say anything, nor does he move toward her*)
LAURA:	You're right. I've been so angry. I haven't seen it before. I've been driving you away, but I need you.
RICHARD:	(*just stands there, unsure*)
LAURA:	I'm angry because my dad died and your dad didn't. It's not even your fault.
RICHARD:	(*brings her to him in a gentle embrace*) I'm so sorry, Laura. I'm so sorry that you hurt. I didn't know.

LAURA: (*pulls back from him*) I was afraid you wouldn't love me, and now you don't love me. I destroyed our picture (*hands torn photo to RICHARD*), and I've destroyed our marriage. You have every right to leave me. (*moves away from him*)

(*RICHARD takes the torn pieces of the photo, holds them, looks to the empty frame, goes to the table where the frame is, puts the torn pieces together in the frame, and places his hand over the remade photo.*)

LAURA: Can you give me some time? Before you make a decision about our marriage?

RICHARD: (*pause, nods*) Take the time that you need, Laura. Take all the time you need.

Opportunities for small group discussion

1. What does anger signal?
2. Do you have unresolved anger? Would others describe you as an angry person?
3. Did you grow up in an angry house? How does that affect your view of conflict?

Resources for further reading

Lerner, Harriet Goldhor. *The Dance of Anger.* New York: Harper and Row, 1985.

Smalley, Gary. *Making Love Last Forever.* Dallas: Word Publishing, 1996.

More great releases from Paul & Nicole Johnson

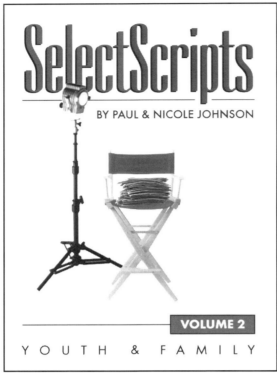

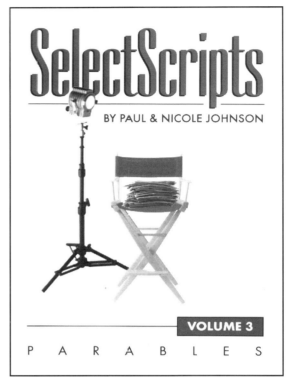

If you've ever been privileged enough to have witnessed this husband-and-wife acting team in action, you know that they leave their audience laughing in the aisles — but also with the lasting impact of how to lead a Christian life. Each volume of *SelectScripts* contains approximately eight scripts. Discussion questions at the end of each script prompt audience participation. Includes suggested resources.

Volume 2: Youth & Family Scripts   0-8054-2024-X
Volume 3: Parable Scripts   0-8054-2025-8

Random Acts of Grace - Dramatic Encounters with God's Love
Two professional actors transfer their inspiring work from stage to page. Ranging from harshly realistic tales of loneliness and despair to imaginative retellings of popular biblical stories, the Johnsons' insights about the nature of people entertain as they encourage spiritual growth. Both humorous and challenging, these stories remind us that even the seemingly random events of life contain the evidence of God's presence.

Trade Book 0-8054-0191-1
Audio Book 0-8054-1775-3

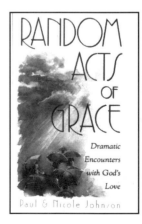

available at fine bookstores everywhere